This book is dedicated to
those who inspire and encourage
our dreams and our dreamers.
Without you, much potential
goes unseen and unrealized.

...and to those who inspire me
every single day.
Ted, Erin, Stephen, Marci,
Sylvia, Rowan and Mom,
you are the Magic in the Mirror.

Deborah A. Battersby

Grandma's Magic Mirror

By Deborah Battersby
Illustrated by Heather Horsley

Grandma came to visit. "Where are my precious grangirls?" she called as she walked in the front door.

She always called her granddaughters her "grangirls".

Grandma dragged a small suitcase on wheels and carried an even smaller case in her hand.

"What's in the little case?" asked Rowan, "I'll show you when we unpack," replied Grandma.

Sylvia and Rowan were quick to help Grandma unpack. They knew a week with Grandma would be filled with surprises.

Then she opened her small case
and showed the girls a mirror.

"Why does it have its own case?"
asked Sylvia.

"Well, it's NOT an ordinary mirror.
It's very special, just like you," said
Grandma. "When you look into this
mirror it gives you a magic message.
It's a special kind of magic that
reminds you what's inside of you.
And it helps you to grow stronger
each day."

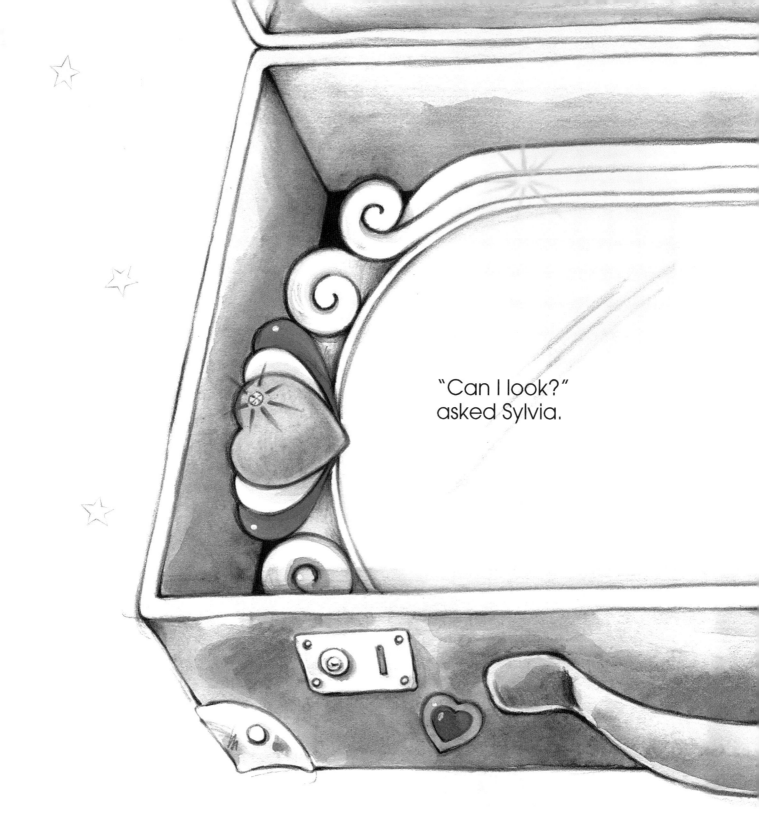

"Can I look?"
asked Sylvia.

"Of course, you can," said Grandma as she handed Sylvia the mirror.

Sylvia looked
into the
mirror

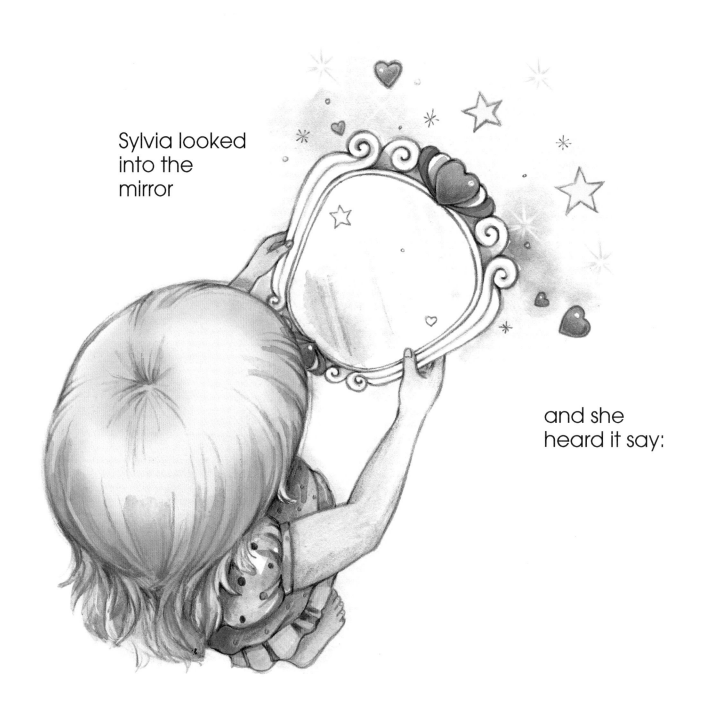

and she
heard it say:

Precious one, you're made of love,
Sparkling like the stars above
Smart and clever brave and strong,
Bright and beautiful all day long

The world is blessed because of you
The things you'll learn, the things you'll do
Your biggest dreams will come to be
When you practice and believe

Remember now… I believe in you
In all you wish, to be, and do
Start the magic, allow; receive
It's fun to practice and believe

A miracle is what you see
With special power yours to weave
Speak the words, the magic spell
I am, I can, I believe!

Sylvia shouted, *"I am, I can, I believe!"*

She giggled and handed the mirror to her little sister.

"Look! Look Rowan!"
she said excitedly.

Rowan smiled and quickly looked into the NOT ordinary mirror and the mirror said:

Precious one, you're made of love,
Sparkling like the stars above
Smart and clever brave and strong,
Bright and beautiful all day long

The world is blessed because of you
The things you'll learn, the things you'll do
Your biggest dreams will come to be
When you practice and believe

Remember now… I believe in you
In all you wish, to be, and do
Start the magic, allow; receive
It's fun to practice and believe

A miracle is what you see
With special power yours to weave
Speak the words, the magic spell
I am, I can, I believe!

Grinning and giggling Rowan shouted
back, *"I am, I can, I believe!"*

Rowan laughed as the girls put their
cheeks together so they could both
look into the mirror at the same time.

The mirror said:

Precious ones, you're made of love,
Sparkling like the stars above
Smart and clever brave and strong,
Bright and beautiful all day long

The world is blessed because of you
The things you'll learn, the things you'll do
Your biggest dreams will come to be
When you practice and believe

Remember now... I believe in you
In all you wish, to be, and do
Start the magic, allow; receive
It's fun to practice and believe

A miracle is what you see
With special power yours to weave
Speak the words, the magic spell
I am, I can, I believe!

Together they chimed
"I am, I can, I believe!"

"Can we use the mirror every day?" the girls asked.

"Yes, of course, every day and more than once a day if you like," said Grandma.

The girls decided to visit the mirror two times each day.

They would look into the mirror in the morning after waking up and in the evening just before bed.

On one of those mornings Rowan came to Grandma with the mirror and her Teddy Bear, Ben, tucked under her arm.

"Grandma do you think the mirror can give Ben a message?"

"I don't know; why do you ask?" she replied.

"He's scared." said Rowan. "What's he scared of?" Grandma inquired.

"He won't try new things. He's afraid he won't do it right and that someone will tease him or make fun of him," said Rowan with a frown. "And that makes him sad."

"Well, let's see what the Magic Mirror has to say."

Rowan held Ben up to the mirror and it said:

> You too are made of love,
> Sparkling like the stars above.
> Rowan loves you, yes indeed.
> It's time to practice and believe
>
> A miracle is what you see
> With special power yours to weave

Speak the words, the magic spell
I am, I can, I believe!

Rowan knew that Ben wouldn't be
afraid anymore.

Sylvia and Rowan visited the mirror
every day during Grandma's stay.

The night before Grandma was to
leave to go home, the girls asked
if they could hear extra messages
from the mirror before going to bed.
Grandma smiled. "Yes, of course,"
She sat with Sylvia and Rowan as they
listened to the mirror's message.

Grandma was a little surprised to
hear the girls saying the messages
to each other along with the mirror.

When they finished Grandma
tucked the girls in and kissed
them good night.
Sylvia and Rowan told Grandma
they loved her and would miss
her and her NOT ordinary mirror.

"I love you and I'll miss you too;
sweet dreams." said Grandma.

When the girls awoke the next
morning Dad had already left to
take Grandma to the airport.

"Grandma has left a message and
a small box for you," said Mom.

The message read:

Dearest grangirls,

Precious ones, you're made of love,
Sparkling like the stars above
Smart and clever brave and strong,
Bright and beautiful all day long

The world is blessed because of you
The things you'll learn, the things you'll do
Your biggest dreams will come to be
When you practice and believe!

Remember now… I believe in you
In all you wish, to be, and do
Start the magic, allow; receive
It's fun to practice and believe

A miracle is what you see
With special power yours to weave
Speak the words, the magic spell
I am, I can, I believe!

This message is magical and its power grows when you share it with others,

the note went on to say:

*Read this message every day;
pass it on along your way.*

Someone needs to hear you to say
the magic words to make their day!

The girls knew what was in the box.

It was Grandma's special and definitely NOT ordinary mirror.

Kids learn a lot from songs. Here's a little treat they're sure to enjoy.

The Magic Mirror Message song, sung to the tune of Twinkle, Twinkle Little Star:

Precious me, I'm made of love,
Sparkling like the stars above,
Smart and clever, brave and strong,
Bright and beautiful all day long

A shining star, that's precious me,
I love my life… and I love me

Fun and kind in every way,
I make a difference every day
All I dream, will be achieved,
When I practice and believe

A shining star, that's precious me;
I am, I can, I believe!

The Grandma Message
Letter to Grownups

Dear Grownup,
(grandparent, parent, teacher, and role model)

Though illustrated through a children's story, this book was written for you. I have long been aware of the power of words to uplift or deflate, inspire or demoralize. Your words not only create your reality they shape the reality of the children and/or impressionable souls around you.

On some level, words of encouragement and discouragement have molded your beliefs about life, about yourself and about what's possible. Knowing this, I wondered, how can we help kids grow their confidence and belief in themselves? What came about is The Grandma Message practice. It is offered here as a strategy for intentionally instilling healthy, empowering beliefs in those you love and influence.

The practice is simple. It's all about telling the children in your world how amazing they are, that they are loved and cared for at all times, and they don't have to do or be anything to earn your love. Tell them they have the power to be, do and have anything they want and all it takes is practice and believing. It also let's them know that achievement usually requires effort. Conditioned belief in their own inner resources will support them throughout their lives.

We throw words around carelessly and do much damage unwittingly. Use your words to encourage, uplift and inspire. Choose to give your amazing gift, the gift of kind, caring empowering words. Every day you can make your words count for good.

You can make a meaningful difference for the children around you. Choose words of encouragement, consistently. Create immediate empowerment as well as long-term positive impact. But here's the secret --- because it is so easy to do it is even easier to NOT do --- so, plan it, make it a daily habit, a priority, like bathing or brushing your teeth.

It'll be one of the most rewarding habits you've ever developed. It makes a great self affirmation too…here's a Grandma Message especially for you:

"You are smart and clever, brave and strong.
You are amazing, gifted and complete.
Today you can make a profound difference.
You can BE and DO anything in the whole wide world.
All it takes is practice and believing.
I believe in you!
I am! I can! I believe!"

Having a strong, positive self-image is priceless, but its greater value shows up in the treatment of others. The better you feel about yourself, the better you treat those around you.

Rowan and Sylvia were three and four when we started the daily phone calls that became The Grandma Messages. Making the calls became a habit. Some days the girls were cranky and didn't want to talk, so I'd leave a voicemail message. They'd sometimes whine, "You always say the same thing, it's boring." Chuckling, I said, "I'll always tell you how amazing you are and how much you're loved." What's funny, though, is that the girls were quick to remind me if I forgot something they particularly liked. Rowan would say, "What about brave, Grandma? We're really, really brave." Sylvia loved 'smart' and 'beautiful' and made sure I always included that part.

Within weeks, the girls started giving Grandma Messages to each other. Sylvia gave one to Rowan when she was crying and didn't want to go to preschool, reminding her how brave and clever she is. Rowan gave several to Sylvia to keep her from quitting in her efforts to cross the monkey bars. "You're strong, practice and believe," she nudged.

Their dad got his share of Grandma Messages too. Once he called home saying he'd be late due to a problem at work. The girls knew what to do. Daddy needed a Grandma Message. Stephen swears it did the trick.

One morning, after a sleep over, Rowan asked to call her mom. Secretly dreading she was going to cry and ask to go home, I handed her the phone only to hear her say, "Hi, Mommy. You're beautiful, brave and smart. You can do anything in the whole wide world. What do we say?" My heart melted, tears streamed down my cheeks; unprompted, a three-year-old was passing it on.

Giving the messages was simple, easy and apparently contagious. I wished I had done this for my children. But wait, they're still my children; I could still do it. So I called them. My husband was next. I called his cell phone and got voicemail. I left his Grandma Message anyway. Three weeks later it was still saved in his voicemail.

Getting sincere words of love and encouragement for NO REASON seemed to appeal to everyone. Even impromptu messages to friends resulted in immediate replies of: you have no idea how much I needed this.

A friend, concerned about her seven-year-old grandson whose parents were divorcing, needed a way to give him extra support. She started her practice; now they're having a great time, enjoying the precious minutes shared each day.

Can mere words help someone feel loved and special? Can your words help the people in your life see their value and worthiness? Can hearing your words of encouragement make a difference to someone you care about? If you believe they can, then join in The Grandma Message project. Empower someone daily with the gift of your words of affirmation. Consider the ripple effect of these messages circulating throughout the world every day. If one life is inspired, you have changed the world for the better.

Let's 'teach the children differently'.

For more inspiration, go to
www.emMatrix.com/giftforgrownups

The Magic Mirror and The Grandma Message

First published in 2010 by Ecademy Press
48 St Vincent Drive, St Albans, Hertfordshire, AL1 5SJ
info@ecademy-press.com www.ecademy-press.com
Printed and Bound by Lightning Source in the UK and USA
Set by Anna Waddell
Illustrated by Heather Horsley

Printed on acid-free paper from managed forests.
This book is printed on demand, so no copies will be remaindered or pulped.
ISBN 978-1-905823-94-9

Made in the USA
Lexington, KY
03 December 2014